JAPANESE AMERICAN
INTERNMENT
CAMPS

Laura Hamilton Waxman

Lerner Publications ◆ Minneapolis

Publisher's note: This book uses the term *internment camp* to describe the confines of Japanese Americans during World War II. Please note that *internment* is often defined in a legal context as the confining of enemy aliens. Because most of the Japanese Americans imprisoned were US citizens, and because they were jailed for their ethnicity, some prefer the term *concentration camp*.

Content consultant: Hana C. Maruyama, PhD student in American Studies, University of Minnesota

Copyright © 2018 by Lerner Publishing Group, Inc.

Lerner Publications Company
An imprint of Lerner Publishing Group, Inc.
241 First Avenue North
Minneapolis, MN 55401 USA

For reading levels and more information, look up this title at www.lernerbooks.com.

Main body text set in Aptifer Slab LT Pro Regular.
Typeface provided by Linotype AG.

Library of Congress Cataloging-in-Publication Data

Names: Waxman, Laura Hamilton, author.
Title: Japanese American internment camps / Laura Hamilton Waxman.
Description: Minneapolis, MN : Lerner Publishing Group, 2018. | Series: Heroes of
    WWII | Audience: Grades 4–6. | Audience: Ages 8–12. | Includes bibliographical
    references and index. | Description based on print version record and CIP data
    provided by publisher; resource not viewed.
Identifiers: LCCN 2017004828 (print) | LCCN 2017010847 (ebook) |
    ISBN 9781512498172 (eb pdf) | ISBN 9781512486438 (lb : alk. paper)
Subjects: LCSH: Japanese Americans—Evacuation and relocation, 1942–1945—
    Juvenile literature. | World War, 1939–1945—Japanese Americans—Juvenile
    literature. | Japanese—United States—History—Juvenile literature.
Classification: LCC D769.8.A6 (ebook) | LCC D769.8.A6 W39 2018 (print) |
    DDC 940.53/1773089956—dc23

LC record available at https://lccn.loc.gov/2017004828

Manufactured in the United States of America
2-52349-33207-6/9/2022

CONTENTS

INTRODUCTION
THE BOMBING HEARD ROUND THE WORLD

On the morning of December 7, 1941, seventeen-year-old Daniel Inouye watched in horror as Japanese fighter planes flew overhead in Hawaii. The planes were headed for a major US naval base in nearby Pearl Harbor.

The fighter planes damaged or destroyed nearly twenty US ships and three hundred military planes. Almost twenty-five hundred sailors, soldiers, and civilians lost their lives that day.

Daniel's parents were Japanese **immigrants**, and they'd taught him to be fiercely loyal to their new country. Daniel had even trained in first aid as a Red Cross volunteer. After the attack, he biked to Pearl Harbor to offer medical help. For days he worked tirelessly to save as many lives as possible.

Smoke rises behind sailors and damaged planes on Ford Island, Pearl Harbor's military base, on the day of the bombing.

News of the bombing traveled fast throughout the United States. A boy named Saburo Masada learned about it while listening to the radio in California. Saburo was shocked that the Japanese would do such a thing. He exclaimed, "Who do they think they are, bombing our country?"

People in San Francisco examine news headlines the day after the Pearl Harbor bombing.

Daniel Inouye earned multiple awards and medals for his military service from 1943 to 1947. He later became a US senator.

For Saburo, Daniel, and thousands of other Japanese Americans, "our country" was the United States. They were deeply distressed by the bombing, just as other Americans were. But Japan had suddenly become enemy number one in the United States, and many Americans suddenly saw Japanese Americans as the enemy. That viewpoint would soon lead to years of imprisonment for many thousands of men, women, and children.

CHAPTER 1
ENEMY NUMBER ONE

Pearl Harbor was attacked during World War II (1939–1945). This conflict had been raging for two years in Europe and other parts of the world. It pitted Germany, Japan, and four other nations against Britain, France, and their **allies**. The day after the bombing, the United States joined Britain and France in the war.

A major cause of World War II was German leader Adolf Hitler's plan to take over Europe. Japanese leaders had been doing something similar in China and Korea. During Hitler's takeover, German soldiers (*far right*) hurt or killed about six million Jews.

Japanese children at Angel Island, an immigration processing center in California, in 1920

BEFORE PEARL HARBOR

Japanese immigrants began to arrive in the United States in the late nineteenth and early twentieth centuries. Many settled on the West Coast, in California, Oregon, and Washington. As immigrants, they were not allowed to become US citizens or to own land. Children born in the United States were automatically citizens.

Like immigrants before them, the Japanese worked hard to make new lives for themselves. But other workers and business owners viewed them as competition. They accused the newcomers of stealing jobs or taking away customers. Eventually the government passed laws preventing more Japanese immigrants from entering the United States.

Masaichi Ishibashi (*left*) and his mother, Take. He was an American citizen born to Japanese immigrant parents soon after they started farming in California in 1910.

EXECUTIVE ORDER 9066

After the attack on Pearl Harbor, **prejudice** and fear toward Japanese Americans exploded. Rumors spread that Japanese Americans were working as spies for Japan. Some Americans worried that the "spies" were planning a Japanese invasion of the West Coast.

Government officials close to President Franklin Roosevelt convinced him that Japanese Americans on the West Coast threatened the country's security. They said that Japanese Americans should be separated from the rest of society.

In February 1942, just two months after the Pearl Harbor attack, Roosevelt issued Executive Order 9066. This official document gave the government the right to remove Japanese Americans from their homes and confine them in **internment** camps, called war **relocation centers** at the time.

This document announcing forced removal of Japanese Americans was posted in California in 1942.

CHAPTER 2
LOSING HOME

Roosevelt's executive order affected all Japanese Americans, even those who were just one-sixteenth Japanese. It affected people who'd been born in Japan. It also affected those born in the United States, who had full citizenship.

The Japanese American owner of this California store put up an I am an American sign the day after the Pearl Harbor attack.

SOLD
BY WHITE & POLLARD

GROCERY WANT

FRUITS
AND
VEGETABLES

I AM AN AMERICAN

WANTO CO.   WANTO CO.

This family waits for their luggage to be inspected before they are sent to an internment camp in 1942.

ONLY WHAT THEY COULD CARRY

Some families learned they'd soon be forced from their homes. They were given just a week to prepare. Others were given only a half day's notice that the government would be transporting them to one of ten relocation centers. These centers were in **remote** parts of California, Arizona, Colorado, Wyoming, Idaho, Utah, and Arkansas.

Families were told to pack "only what you can carry." Everything else had to be sold or left behind. Sixteen-year-old Ernest Uno had worked hard to earn money

The Mochida family of California wears tags meant to keep them together as they travel to an internment camp.

for his shiny red-and-white bicycle. He sold it for only five dollars. "It broke my heart that that was all it was worth to whoever bought it," he recalled.

LOSING IT ALL

Ernest wasn't alone. Many individuals and families were forced to sell their property and possessions. In their desperation, they often accepted unfairly low prices.

A young California businessman named Frank Emi ran his family's supermarket. He had just spent his entire savings of $25,000 on new updates. He was forced to sell the store and everything in it for just $1,500.

By the end of the week, he and other Japanese Americans were expected to gather at an appointed location. From there, they would be transported away. Eleven-year-old Ben Tateishi from San Diego saw white neighbors peeking out of curtains as he and his family left their home. His neighbors' silent staring filled him with shame.

Sally Tsuneishi passed her high school as she left Los Angeles. "I thought of the prize-winning essay that I had written for my high school English class," she remembered. "It was entitled, 'Why I am Proud to Be an American.'" Tears streamed down her face as she realized that her country now viewed her as the enemy.

HERO HIGHLIGHT

During the war, the US government asked Japanese American men to fill out a form to prove their loyalty to the country. It included questions about the men's willingness to serve in the US military. Those who replied no to those questions became known as No-No Boys. Some of these young men, including Noboru Taguma (*right*), were jailed for their supposedly disloyal answers.

CHAPTER 3
THE RELOCATION CENTERS

Buses and trains took more than 110,000 Japanese Americans to the relocation centers. Making matters worse, the FBI had been arresting some Japanese Americans, believing them to be a danger to the country. So while most families stayed together, many traveled without one or both parents.

Japanese Americans from Los Angeles board a train bound for California's Manzanar War Relocation Center.

Manzanar was in California's Owens Valley, between the Sierra Nevada and Inyo Mountains.

ARRIVAL

Many of the relocation centers were in harsh desert climates. They were surrounded by sharp barbed wire fences. Guards kept watch, and anyone who tried to escape would be shot.

A young boy named John Y. Tateishi clung to his parents as his family entered a large relocation center in California called Manzanar. "We looked up at guard towers and felt a deep fear of armed soldiers who stood guard over us," he remembers.

Families were crowded into cramped, poorly built **barracks** with thin **tar paper** walls. The barracks had no plumbing or cooking stoves. They did have small heating stoves, but those barely kept out the nighttime cold. Illness and disease in these close quarters spread easily from person to person.

Internment Camps in the United States

CANADA

IDAHO

WYOMING

CALIFORNIA

Topaz

UTAH

COLORADO

UNITED STATES

Manzanar

ARIZONA

Gila River

ARKANSAS

MEXICO

- ■ Internment camp
- -·--·-- International border
- ▦ State border
- ■ State with internment camp

Toyo Suyemoto and her family were assigned to a barrack at Topaz in Utah. The small room was empty except for a few army cots and mattresses. The floor was covered in a thick layer of dust. Before moving in, Toyo's family borrowed brooms to sweep it clean.

MAKING THE BEST
OF A BAD SITUATION

Internees found other ways to make their barracks
more inviting. They built shelves and furniture
from scraps of wood. From scraps of cloth, they made
curtains for windows and showers. Before then,
nothing even separated neighbors' bathrooms. Some
families built dividing walls out of wood and cloth.
That way, they could have some privacy.

Outside, some people managed to build simple
wooden playgrounds. Others started Japanese gardens.
In these ways, they made the harsh barracks a little
more like homes.

STEM HIGHLIGHT

One key job at the relocation
centers was farming. By the
end of 1943, the centers were
growing 85 percent of their own
vegetables. They also raised farm
animals such as hogs, chickens,
and cattle. Gila River in Arizona
even ran its own dairy farm.

CHAPTER 4
DAILY LIFE

Life was difficult in the internment camps. Feeling homesick was just one of many challenges of living behind guarded fences.

   Most adults had paying jobs. There were positions for doctors, nurses, teachers, cleaners, cooks, office workers, and much more. The men and women were paid a fraction of what they would have earned back home. But the work allowed them to earn a bit of money. They could purchase extras at camp stores or save these small amounts for the day they left the camps.

A family in their small living space at the Tule Lake camp

Many adults struggled to adapt to their new life. They missed earning a good living and supporting their families. Young Charles Kikuchi's father was often sad. He rarely left their barracks. But Charles's mother experienced a new sense of community. Back home, she'd had a more traditional role as caretaker of the household. At Gila River, she enjoyed getting out more and making new friends.

STEM HIGHLIGHT

A few talented chemists and **botanists** were able to use their skills to help the United States. For instance, rubber was in short supply because of the war. It was used for vehicle tires, among other things. At Manzanar, Japanese American scientists experimented with a plant called guayule (*right*), to make a new kind of rubber. It was as strong as traditional rubber. Still, the government didn't give the scientists much credit for their work.

SCHOOL AND FUN

Like their parents, children had to get used to a new life. Many longed to return home to old friends and neighbors. Some children found a little comfort in being surrounded by so many young people.

During the day, children went to school in barracks divided into small classrooms. They studied subjects such as art, science, languages, social studies, music, and math.

Staying busy helped keep the homesickness at bay.

A fourth-grade class at Rohwer camp in Arkansas in 1942

Women's basketball games often drew big crowds at Manzanar.

In their free time, children joined the Boy Scouts and Girl Scouts, and adults ran newspapers.

Sports were also popular. People made baseball diamonds and formed baseball leagues. In the fall, they played football and basketball. Some players were even recruited to college or professional teams.

CHAPTER 5
STARTING OVER

In December 1944, the Supreme Court made an important ruling. It stated that the US government did not have the right to imprison people who had done nothing wrong. That month the government announced that it would start closing the internment camps. Between 1945 and 1946, internees were allowed to return home.

A camp officer checks names off a list as Japanese Americans prepare to leave Gila River in Arizona in September 1945.

The Supreme Court case that led to the closing of the internment camps was fought on behalf of Mitsuye Endo (*right*). She stood for all the innocent Japanese Americans who were imprisoned.

NO HOME TO RETURN TO

Most people returned home to nothing. Mitsuo Usui's father had sold his California plant nursery to a neighbor for $1,000. The neighbor agreed that he could buy it back for a similar price when he returned. But Mitsuo's family discovered that the neighbor had sold their property to another man. This man demanded a price of $26,000. The family did not have that kind of money. They lost everything.

A few lucky families had kinder neighbors. In Sacramento, California, Bob Fletcher promised to look after the farms of the Nitto, Okamoto, and Tsukamoto families. In return, they agreed he could keep half of the profits. When they came home, their land was well cared for and waiting for them.

AN APOLOGY

Japanese Americans had lost their property and dignity. They had been treated as enemies by the country they loved. Yet the government refused to apologize or pay them back for their losses.

In the 1960s, Japanese Americans launched a movement to demand justice. Finally, in 1988, the US Congress agreed to pay every living internee $20,000. This money would help to make up for what Japanese Americans had lost. The government also issued an apology for how it had treated Japanese Americans during the war.

The US attorney general (*right*) gives payments to Japanese Americans in 1990, more than forty years after internment.

Edison Uno (*right*) was thirteen when he, his parents, and his nine siblings were forced from their home. They lived at relocation centers in Colorado and Texas. In the 1960s and 1970s, Uno led a **redress** movement to demand justice from the government. He gave speeches, served in local government, taught classes, and consulted on books and movies about the internment camps.

Since then Americans have come to realize the injustice of the internment camps. Many have vowed to never allow such a thing to happen to any group of people in the United States again.

TIMELINE

1885	A wave of Japanese immigrants begins arriving in the United States, but the US government refuses to grant them citizenship. Only Japanese Americans born in the United States are considered citizens.
1913	The First Alien Land Law is passed in California. It bans anyone born in Japan from owning land. Other states soon passed similar laws.
1924	The Immigration Act of 1924 blocks new Japanese immigrants from entering the United States.
September 1, 1939	World War II begins in Europe. Conflicts were already under way there and in Asia.
December 7, 1941	Japanese fighter planes attack the Pearl Harbor naval base in Hawaii.
December 8, 1941	President Roosevelt declares war on Japan, and the United States enters World War II. The FBI arrests more than one thousand Japanese American men.

1942	President Roosevelt signs Executive Order 9066 on February 19. By spring about 110,000 Japanese Americans have been forced into internment camps.
December 1944	The US Supreme Court rules in Ex Parte Endo that the US government cannot imprison people who have been proven to be loyal to the United States. The government begins to shut down the relocation centers.
September 2, 1945	World War II ends.
1960s	The redress movement begins. Its leaders demand an apology from the US government and payment for the losses that Japanese Americans suffered.
August 10, 1988	President Ronald Reagan signs a new law that gives $20,000 and a government apology to each surviving internee. The law also sets up a fund to educate Americans about the dangers of prejudice.
1990s	Japanese Americans who were imprisoned in the relocation centers receive payments from the government.

Source Notes

6 Tammy Real-McKeighan, "Couple Shares Story of Living in Japanese Internment Camps," *Fremont (NE) Tribune*, April 24, 2012, http://fremonttribune.com/news/local/couple-shares-story-of-living-in-japanese-internment-camps/article_f917df1e-8e20-11e1-bbc4-001a4bcf887a.html.

13 Richard Reeves, *Infamy: The Shocking Story of the Japanese American Internment in World War II* (New York: Henry Holt, 2015), 66.

14 Ellen Levine, *A Fence Away from Freedom: Japanese Americans and World War II* (G. P. Putnam's Sons, 1995), 35.

15 Reeves, *Infamy*, 76–77.

17 Erica Harth, ed. *Last Witness: Reflections on the Wartime Internment of Japanese Americans* (New York: Palgrave, 2001), 129.

Glossary

allies: in wartime, nations fighting together against a common enemy

barracks: a set of simple buildings usually used to house soldiers

botanists: scientists who study and work with plants

immigrants: people who move to another country to live permanently

internees: people confined to an internment camp

internment: confinement as a prisoner, especially during wartime

prejudice: an unfair judgment or opinion not based on facts

redress: to make up for a wrong or an injustice

relocation centers: areas where Japanese Americans were imprisoned in the United States during World War II. Relocation centers were often called internment camps.

remote: far away and isolated

tar paper: a heavy black paper coated in a thick substance called tar

FURTHER INFORMATION

Bailey, Rachel A. *The Japanese Internment Camps.* Ann Arbor, MI: Cherry Lake, 2014.

Children of the Camps: Internment History
http://www.pbs.org/childofcamp/history/index.html

Japanese American National Museum
http://www.janm.org

Japanese American Relocation Videos
http://www.history.com/topics/world-war-ii/japanese-american -relocation/videos/japanese-internment-in-america

Japanese American WWII Incarceration: The Core Story
http://www.densho.org/core-story/

Our Story: Daily Life in the Internment Camps
http://amhistory.si.edu/ourstory/activities/internment/more.html

Owens, Lisa L. *Attack on Pearl Harbor.* Minneapolis: Lerner Publications, 2018.

Sullivan, Laura L. *Life as a Child in a Japanese Internment Camp.* New York: Cavendish Square, 2017.

Index

Photo Acknowledgments

The images in this book are used with the permission of: © iStockphoto.
com/akinshin (barbed wire backgrounds throughout); © iStockphoto.
com/ElementalImaging, p. 1 (camouflage background); National Archives,
pp. 4–5, 11, 12, 13, 14, 16, 19, 20, 21, 22, 23, 24, 25, 29; Library of Congress
(LC-USF34-081814-E), p. 6; AP Photo, p. 7; United States Holocaust Memorial
Museum, courtesy of National Archives and Records Administration, College
Park, pp. 8, 28; © Bettmann/Getty Images, p. 9; Department of Archives
and Special Collections, California State University Dominguez Hills, p. 10;
© iStockphoto.com/aaron007, pp. 15, 27 (barbed wire frame); Sacramento
State University Library, p. 15; Library of Congress (LC-DIG-ppprs-00338),
p. 17; © Laura Westlund/Independent Picture Service, p. 18; AP Photo/Dennis
Cook, p. 26; Courtesy of UCSF Archives & Special Collections, p. 27.

Cover: National Archives (child); © iStockphoto.com/akinshin (barbed
wire background); © iStockphoto.com/ElementalImaging (camouflage
background); © iStockphoto.com/MillefloreImages (flag background).